PHILIP'S *Red Books*

COUNTY STREET ATLAS

DORSET

44 TOWN CENTRE STR...

ROAD MAPS PAGE LAYOUT

[Road map page layout showing a map of the region around Dorset with page grid references: 8-9, 10-11, 12-13, 14-15, with place names including Abercarn, Cwmbran, Chepstow, Stone, Wotton-under-Edge, Tetbury, Cricklade, Faringdon, Risca, Alveston, Highworth, Caerphilly, NEWPORT, Almondsbury, Malmesbury, Swindon, Wantage, CARDIFF, Avonmouth, Chipping Sodbury, Wootton Bassett, Ashbury, Portishead, BRISTOL, Marshfield, Aldbourne, Great Shefford, Penarth, Clevedon, Chippenham, Calne, Hungerford, Barry, Congresbury, Nailsea, Box, Beckhampton, Marlborough, Bath, Melksham, Devizes, Highclere, Weston-super-Mare, Sandford, Blagdon, Radstock, Trowbridge, Pewsey, Burbage, East Brent, Midsomer Norton, Upavon, Hurstbourne Tarrant, Burnham-on-Sea, Cheddar, Frome, Ludgershall, Weyhill, Wells, Shepton Mallet, Warminster, Andover, Glastonbury, Evercreech, Heytesbury, Amesbury, Bishop's Lydeard, Bridgwater, Street, Castle Cary, Bruton, Mere, Wylye, Wilton, Stockbridge, Othery, Wincanton, East Knoyle, Salisbury, Taunton, Langport, Gillingham, Swallowcliffe, Sparkford, Shaftesbury, Whiteparish, Romsey, Broadway, Ilminster, Yeovil, Stalbridge, Iwerne, Sixpenny Hanley, Fordingbridge, Cadnam, Culmstock, Crewkerne, Sturminster Newton, Minster, SOUTHAMPTON, Yarcombe, Chard, Yetminster, Blandford Forum, Ringwood, Lyndhurst, Chardstock, Beaminster, Cerne Abbas, Spetisbury, Wimborne Minster, Brockenhurst, Honiton, Axminster, Frampton, Bere Regis, Ottery St Mary, Bridport, Puddletown, BOURNEMOUTH, Lymington, Seaton, Lyme Regis, Dorchester, Poole, Christchurch, Sidmouth, Broadmayne, Wareham, Corfe Castle, Isle of Wight, Weymouth, Swanage, Fortuneswell]

www.philips-maps.co.uk

This edition published by Philip's,
a division of Octopus Publishing Group Ltd
www.octopusbooks.co.uk
2–4 Heron Quays, London E14 4JP
An Hachette Livre UK Company
www.hachettelivre.co.uk

First published in 1980 by Estate Publications
First Philip's edition 2008
First impression 2008
11/08-06

ISBN 978-0-540-09471-4

© Philip's 2008

This product includes mapping data licensed
from Ordnance Survey®, with the permission
of the Controller of Her Majesty's Stationery
Office.© Crown copyright 2006. All rights
reserved. Licence number 100011710

ROAD MAPPING

1 : 200,000 - 3.16 Miles to 1 Inch

```
0       2       4       6       8       10      12      14      16 Kilometres
0           2           4           6           8           10 Miles
```

M6	Motorway
23	Motorway Junction
22	Motorway Junction (Restricted Access)
S	Motorway Service Area
=====	Motorway Under Construction
A40	Primary Route (Dual Carriageway)
A49	Primary Route (Single Carriageway)
S	Non Motorway Service Area
	Narrow Primary Route
=====	Primary Route (Under Construction)
6	Distance in Miles

A379	'A' Road (Dual Carriageway)
A387	'A' Road (Single Carriageway)
A897	Narrow 'A' Road
A387	'A' Road (Under Construction)
B4568	'B' Road (Dual Carriageway)
B4385	'B' Road (Single Carriageway)
B873	Narrow 'B' Road
=====	'B' Road (Under Construction)
	Minor Road
●	Railway with Station
●—	Tourist Railway with Station

●○○○●	Roundabouts
– · – · –	National Boundary
– · · – · · –	County Boundary
	Built Up Area
	Canal
	Lake / Reservoir & River
	Coastal Area and Beach
	National Scenic Area / National Park
	Woodland
– – – – –	National Trail
12	Adjoining Pages

TOURIST SYMBOLS on road maps

✈	Airport	▦	Entertainment Centre	🏛	Prehistoric Monument
🚢	Hovercraft	✿	Garden		Roman Remains
🛳	Hydrofoil	⚑9 ⚑18	Golf Courses (9 & 18 holes)	🦅	RSPB Reserve
⚓	Passenger Ferry	⚑	Golf Driving Range, Pitch & Putt		Ski Slope Centre
🚢	Seacat		Holiday Centre		Sub Aqua Activity
🚗 🚢	Vehicle Ferries	🏇	Horse Racing	⚓	Surfing
		🏠	House / Building of Interest		Theatre
❋	Ancient Fort	🏛	House and Garden	i	Tourist Information Centre
🐾	Animal Attraction		Industrial Interest	i	(Seasonal)
🐟	Aquarium	🌳	Leisure / Theme Park	i	(National Trust, National Park)
✕	Battle Site	🏯	Lighthouse		Tourist Railway
🌉	Bridge of Interest	▲	Monument, Folly	☀	Viewpoint
⛺	Camping Site		Motorsports Centre / Venue	🍇	Vineyard & Cider Producer
⊘	Caravan Club Site	🏛	Museum / Art Gallery		Water Skiing
🚐	Caravan Site	🌿	National Nature Reserve	🏭	Watermill
🏰	Castle, Tower	●	National Trail	⚐	Wildlife Park
✝	Cathedral, Abbey, Priory	★	Other Place of Interest	✕	Windmill
🏛	Church of Interest	⊕	Outdoor Pursuits	🏭	Working Farm
🏛	Country Park	🪑	Picnic Site	▲	Youth Hostel
✈	Craft Centre	🐚	Place of Natural Beauty	🐘	Zoo

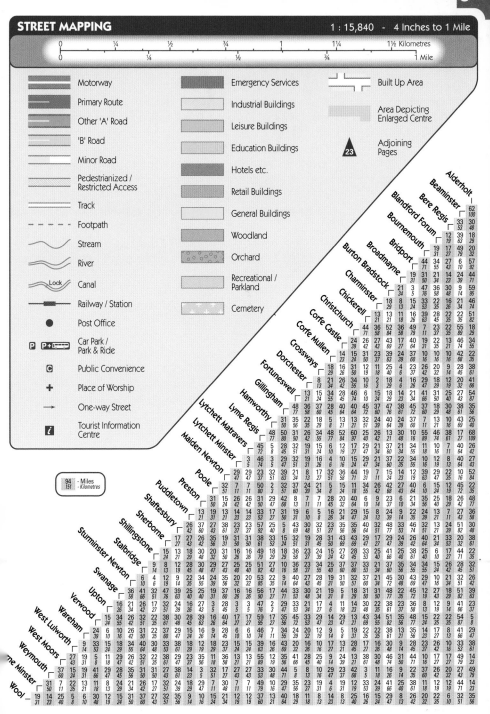

STREET MAPPING

1 : 15,840 - 4 Inches to 1 Mile

- Motorway
- Primary Route
- Other 'A' Road
- 'B' Road
- Minor Road
- Pedestrianized / Restricted Access
- Track
- Footpath
- Stream
- River
- Lock — Canal
- Railway / Station
- Post Office
- Car Park / Park & Ride
- Public Convenience
- Place of Worship
- One-way Street
- Tourist Information Centre

- Emergency Services
- Industrial Buildings
- Leisure Buildings
- Education Buildings
- Hotels etc.
- Retail Buildings
- General Buildings
- Woodland
- Orchard
- Recreational / Parkland
- Cemetery

- Built Up Area
- Area Depicting Enlarged Centre
- Adjoining Pages

94 - Miles
151 - Kilometres

Blandford Forum 19 B5	1 Greyhound Yd, Market Pl, Blandford Forum, DT11 7EB Tel: 01258 454770 Email: blandfordtic@north-dorset.gov.uk
Bournemouth 20 C5	Westover Rd, Bournemouth, BH1 2BU Tel: 01202 451700 Email: info@bournemouth.gov.uk
Bridport 22 C4	47 South St, Bridport, DT6 3NY Tel: 01308 424901 Email: bridport.tic@westdorset-dc.gov.uk
Christchurch 28 B4	49 High St, Christchurch, BH23 1AS Tel: 01202 471780 Email: enquiries@christchurchtourism.info
Dorchester 31 E3	11 Antelope Walk, Dorchester, DT1 1BE Tel: 01305 267992 Email: dorchester.tic@westdorset-dc.gov.uk
Lyme Regis 35 E3	Guildhall Cottage, Church St, Lyme Regis, DT7 3BS Tel: 01297 442138 Email: lymeregis.tic@westdorset-dc.gov.uk
Poole Welcome Centre 38 B6	Enefco House, Poole Quay, Poole, BH15 1HJ Tel: 01202 253253 Email: info@poole.gov.uk
Shaftesbury 40 C3	8 Bell St, Shaftesbury, SP7 8AE Tel: 01747 853514 Email: shaftesburytic@north-dorset.gov.uk
Sherborne 41 D3	3 Tilton Ct, Digby Rd, Sherborne, DT9 3NL Tel: 01935 815341 Email: sherborne.tic@westdorset-dc.gov.uk
Swanage 45 G4	The White House, Shore Rd, Swanage, BH19 1LB Tel: 01929 422885 Email: mail@swanage.gov.uk
Wareham 50 B6	Holy Trinity Church, South St, Wareham, BH20 4LU Tel: 01929 552740 Email: tic@purbeck-dc.gov.uk
Weymouth & Portland 55 F1	The King's Statue, The Esplanade, Weymouth, DT4 7AN Tel: 01305 785747 Email: tic@weymouth.gov.uk
Wimborne Minster 57 B3	29 High St, Wimborne Minster, BH21 1HR Tel: 01202 886116 Email: wimbornetic@eastdorset.gov.uk

This **COUNTY STREET ATLAS** contains street maps for each town centre.
The street atlases listed below are **LOCAL STREET ATLASES**,
with comprehensive local coverage.

BOURNEMOUTH

including: Barton on Sea, Bearwood, Boscombe, Bransgore, Burton, Christchurch, Everton, Ferndown, Hamworthey, Highcliffe, Hordle, Merley, Milford on Sea, Mudeford, New Milton, Poole, Ringwood, St Ives, St Leonards, Sandbanks, Sway, Upton, Verwood, West Moors, Wimborne Minster etc.

NEW FOREST

including: Ashurst, Barton on Sea, Beaulieu, Bransgore, Brockenhurst, Burley, Cadnam, Christchurch, Dibden Purlieu, Everton, Fawley, Fordingbridge, Hammonds Green, Highcliffe, Hordle, Hythe, Lymington, Lyndhurst, Milford on Sea, Mudeford, New Milton, Ringwood, Sway, Totton etc.

WEYMOUTH & DORCHESTER

including: Broadmayne, Charlestown, Charminster, Chickerell, Crossways, Dorchester, Easton, Fortuneswell, Martinstown, Preston, Puddletown, Radipole, Southlands, Southwell, Upwey, West Stafford, Wyke Regis etc.

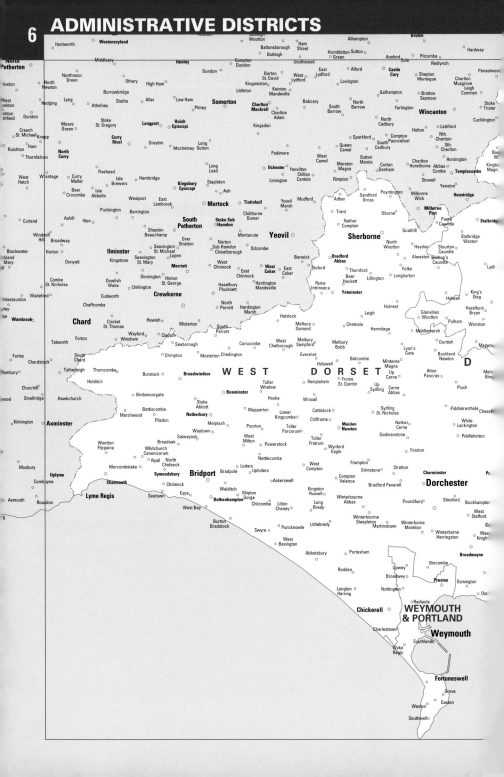

Stourton · Mere · Chicklade · Berwick St Leonard · Fonthill Bishop · Langford · Teffont Magna · Great Wishford · Stoford · Woodford · Lower Woodford · Winterbourne Dauntsey · Winterbourne Gunner · Gunville

Zeals · West Knoyle · Hindon · Chilmark · Teffont Evias · Chicksgrove · Dinton · Baverstock · South Newton · Wilton · Bemerton Heath · Firsdown · Middle Winterslow

Ilton · Milton on Stour · Gillingham · Sedgehill · Semley · Newtown · Hatch · Tisbury · Sutton Mandeville · Fovant · Compton Chamberlayne · Barford St. Martin · Burcombe · Netherhampton · Harnham · **Salisbury** · Laverstock · Pitton · Farley · West Winterslow · The Common · West Tytherley

Wyke · Motcombe · Swallowcliffe · Broad Chalke · Bishopstone · Coombe Bissett · Stratford Tony · Odstock · Homington · Nunton · Bodenham · Whaddon · Alderbury · Britford · West Grimstead · East Grimstead · West Dean · East Dean

West Stour · East Stour · **Shaftesbury** · Ludwell · Cann Common · Charlton · Alvediston · Ebbesbourne Wake · Bowerchalke · Woodminton · Wick · Downton · Morgan's Vale Woodfalls · Charlton-All-Saints · Whiteparish

Stour Provost · Stour Row · Guy's Marsh · Cann Marsh · Melbury Abbas · Berwick St. John · Woodyates · Martin Drove End · Martin · Tidpit · Whitsbury · Nth. Charford · Hale · **Redlynch** · Lover · Landford · Landford Manor

Todber · Margaret Marsh · Compton Abbas · Ashmore · Tollard Royal · Deanland · Sixpenny Handley · Pentridge · Rockbourne · Upper Street · Breamore · Woodgreen · Nomansland · Plai

arnhull · West Orchard · Fontmell Magna · Sutton Waldron · Manston · Farnham · Dean · Monkton Up Wimborne · Damerham · Sandleheath · **Fordingbridge** · Godshill · Bramshaw

Hinton St. Mary · **Sturminster Newton** · Hammoon · Iwerne Minster · Stubhampton · Chettle · Cashmoor · Wimborne St Giles · Cranborne · Edmondsham · **Alderholt** · Stuckton · Blissford · Fritham · Brook

Fiddleford · Child Okeford · Iwerne Courtney or Shroton · Tarrant Gunville · Tarrant Hinton · Gussage St. Michael · Gussage All Saints · **EAST DORSET** · Bickton · Hyde · North Gorley · Stoney Cross

Broad Oak · Okeford Fitzpaine · **Shillingstone** · Stourpaine · Pimperne · Long Crichel · Woodlands · **Verwood** · Ibsley · South Gorley

Ibberton · Turnworth · Durweston · Blandford Camp · More Crichel · Manswood · Horton · Wigbeth · Three Legged Cross · Blashford · Linford · Mockbeggar · Linwood

NORTH DORSET · Bryanston · Blandford St. Mary · **Blandford Forum** · Tarrant Rawston · Tarrant Rushton · Witchampton · Hinton Martell · Chalbury Common · Mannington · Ashley Heath · **St Ives** · Avon Castle · Burley Street · Picket Post · **Ringwood** · Burley

Winterborne Houghton · Winterborne Stickland · Winterborne Clenston · Charlton Marshall · Tarrant Keyneston · Tarrant Crawford · Stanbridge · Gaunt's Common · Holt · St Leonards · Kingston · Burley · Bisterne Close · Brocken

Milton Abbas · Whatcombe · Winterborne Whitechurch · Thorncombe · Spetisbury · Shapwick · Tadden · Clappate · Broom Hill · **West Moors** · **Colehill** · **Wimborne Minster** · Hampreston · Merley · Longham · **West Parley** · Parley Cross · Trickett's Cross · Thorney Hill · Avon · Ripley · Sopley · Neacroft · **Bransgore** · **Sway** · Wootton · Bashley

Milborne St. Andrew · Winterborne Kingston · Winterborne Zelston · Anderson · Almer · **Sturminster Marshall** · **Corfe Mullen** · East End · Bearwood · Ensbury · **Ferndown** · Hurn · **CHRISTCHURCH** · Hinton · Highcliffe · **New Milton** · Barton on Sea

Tolpuddle · Turners Puddle · Affpuddle · **Bere Regis** · Bloxworth · West Morden · East Morden · **Lytchett Matravers** · **Broadstone** · Moordown · Burton · Mudeford

Briantspuddle · Slepe · **Lytchett Minster** · **Upton** · Waterloo · Newtown · Winton · **POOLE** · **BOURNEMOUTH** · Southbourne · **Christchurch** · Mid on

Holton Heath · Hamworthy · Branksome · Westbourne · Boscombe · **Poole** · Parkstone · Branksome Park · **Bournemouth**

Moreton · Bovington Camp · Sandford · **Wareham** · Holton Heath · Barkley Sands

East Burton · Stokeford · **Wool** · Stoborough · Ridge · Arne · Sandbank

East Knighton · East Stoke · West Holme · Stoborough Green · **PURBECK**

Winfrith Newburgh · Coombe Keynes · Furzebrook · Norden · Studland

ton Herring · st Chaldon · West Lulworth · East Lulworth · East Creech · Church Knowle · **Corfe Castle** · Langton Matravers

Tyneham · Steeple · Kingston · Harman's Cross · Kimmeridge · **Swanage**

Worth Matravers

St. Aldhelm's or St. Alban's Head

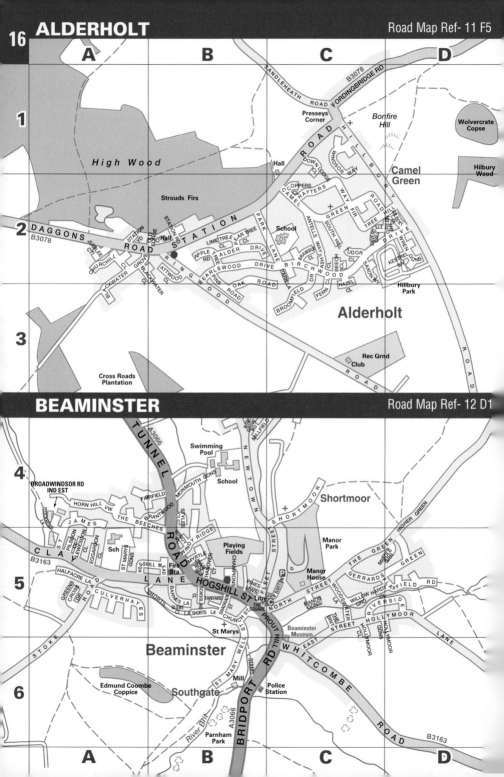

ALDERHOLT

A B C D

1

High Wood

B3078 FORDINGBRIDGE RD

SANDLEHEATH ROAD

Presseys Corner

Bonfire Hill

Wolvercrate Copse

ROAD

Hall

DOWN LODGE CL

WINDSOR WAY

HILLBURY

Camel Green

Hilbury Wood

Strouds Firs

COPPERS

CAMEL

CLAYTERS CL

GREEN FIR

ROAD

TREE

HILL

2

DAGGONS

B3078

Station Yd

Hall

ROAD

STATION

Station Rd

RING WOOD

ATTWOOD

JUBILEE

CHURCHILL

GROVE

BLACKWATER

BLACKWATER

PARK LANE

LIME TREE CL

PEAR TREE CL

ALDER DRIVE

APPLE RD

EARLSWOOD

PINE ROAD

OAK ROAD

DRIVE

PIERLA

BIRCHWOOD

School

ANTELLS WAY

SOUTH HILL

BRAMBLE CL

DR

BROOMFIELD

FERN

BEECH

HAZEL CL

WOOD

TUDOR CL

SAXON WAY

KESTREL GDNS

WREN CL

DRIVE

Hillbury Park

Alderholt

3

Cross Roads Plantation

ROAD

Rec Grnd

Club

ROAD

BEAMINSTER

TUNNEL

A3066

BOOKSHOP GRO

HILLFIELD

4

BROADWINDSOR RD IND EST

Swimming Pool

School

NEWTOWN

SHORTMOOR

Shortmoor

HORN HILL

FAIRFIELD

MONMOUTH GDNS

BRANTWOOD

STYLES

ROAD

THE BEECHES

JAMES ST

PILSDON

LEWESDON

EGGARDON

Sch

WINDY RIDGE

ST MARYS GDNS

SHILL MEAD

MYRTLE

HANOVER

CHAMPIONS

Playing Fields

Manor Park

HIGHER GREEN

THE GREEN

GERRARDS

MIDDLE GDNS

MAXFIELD

GREEN

RD

5

B3163

CLAY

HALFACRE LA

GREENS CROSS DR

CULVERHAYES

SHORTS

BARNES LA

GLEBE

LA SHORTS LA

TANYARD

SHADRACK

CHURCH ST

ST MARY WELL ST

HOGSHILL ST

PINES MWS

ST

FLEET

NORTH ST

THE SQUARE

Liby

Fire Sta

Manor House

MANOR GDNS

MANOR ST

WOODWATER

WILLOW HARDY

GRO

HOLLYMOOR

RIVERSIDE

HOLLYMOOR GDNS

HOLLYMOOR LANE

6

STOKE

Beaminster

St Marys

Edmund Coombe Coppice

Southgate

ST MARY WELL ST

Mill

PROUT HILL RD

EAST ST

Beaminster Museum

THE BRIT

Police Station

WHITCOMBE

ROAD

B3163

River Brit

BRIDPORT RD

A3066

Parnham Park

A B C D

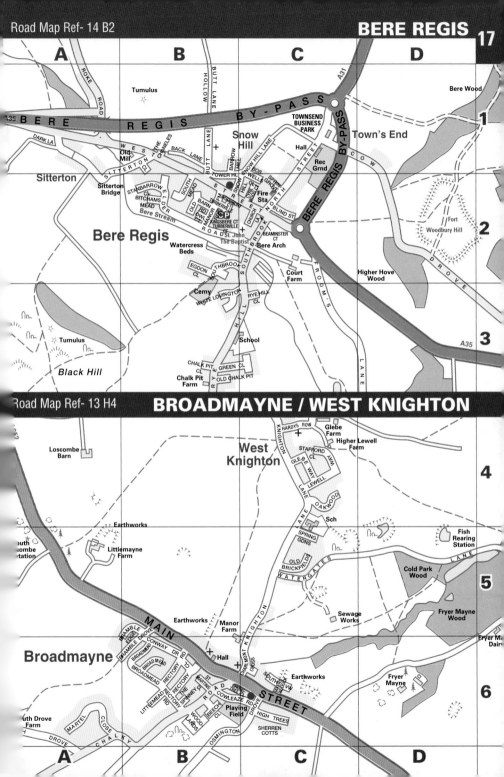

A   B   C   D

Tumulus

Bere Wood

ROKE ROAD

BUTT LANE

HOLLOW LANE

BERE   REGIS   BY-PASS

A31

1

BERE

A35

DARK LA

WEST CHALDES

BACK LANE

BUTT LANE

Snow Hill

TOWNSEND BUSINESS PARK

Town's End

BERE REGIS BY-PASS

COW

Old Mill

SITTERTON ROAD

SOUTH MEAD

OLD BARN

SNOW HILL

SNOW HILL LANE

Hall

STREET

SPRING

WELLS

Rec Grnd

Sitterton

Sitterton Bridge

STANBARROW CL

BITCHAMS MEAD

ELDERS MEAD

MANOR RD

Bere Stream

KINGSBERE CT TURBERVILLE

TURBERVILLE CT

CHURCH LA

Fire Sta

ROBLIND ST

DROVE

2

Bere Regis

OLD BARN

St. John The Baptist

BEAMINSTER CT

Bere Arch

Fort

Woodbury Hill

Watercress Beds

SOUTHBROOK

EGDON CL

SOUTH

Court Farm

FROOM'S

Higher Hove Wood

Cemy

WHITE LOVINGTON

RYE HILL CL

HILL

LANE

3

Tumulus

School

A35

Black Hill

CHALK PIT CL

GREEN CL

OLD CHALK PIT

Chalk Pit Farm

Loscombe Barn

HARDYS ROW

Glebe Farm

Higher Lewell Farm

KNIGHTON

West Knighton

STAFFORD AVM

GLEBE CL

LEWELL WAY

LANE

4

Earthworks

OAKWOOD

Sch

South combe Station

Littlemayne Farm

LANE

SPRING GDNS

Fish Rearing Station

OLD BRICKFIELD

WATERGATES

Cold Park Wood

LANE

5

MAIN ST

Earthworks

Manor Farm

KNIGHTON

Sewage Works

Fryer Mayne Wood

Fryer M. Dair

Broadmayne

BRAMBLE EDGE

BRAMBLE DROVE

CONWAY DR

BROADMEAD

RECTORY RD

CHARLMONT CROSS

SOUTHERN DROVE

Earthworks

Fryer Mayne

BROAD MEAD

LITTLEMEAD RD

RECTORY RD

ST MARTINS RD

THE SPINNEY

BEECH CL

WOOD LANE

Hall

COWLEAZE RD

STREET

HIGH TREES

uth Drove Farm

MARTEL CLOSE

CHALKY RD

DROVE

OSMINGTON RD

Playing Field

SHERREN COTTS

6

A   B   C   D

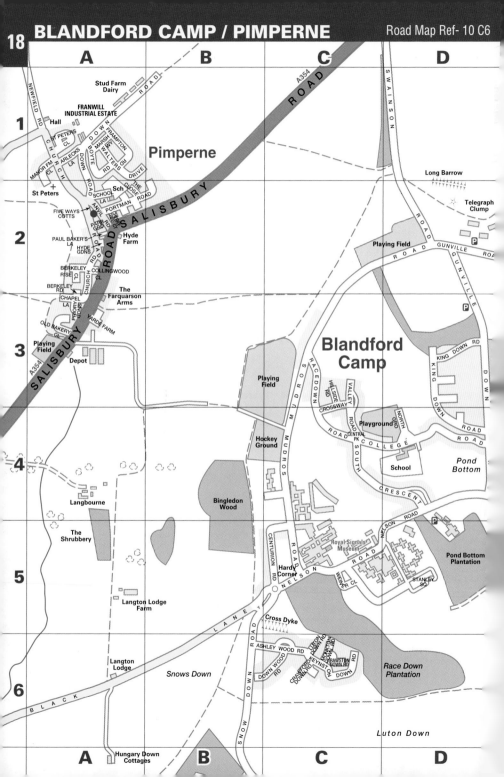

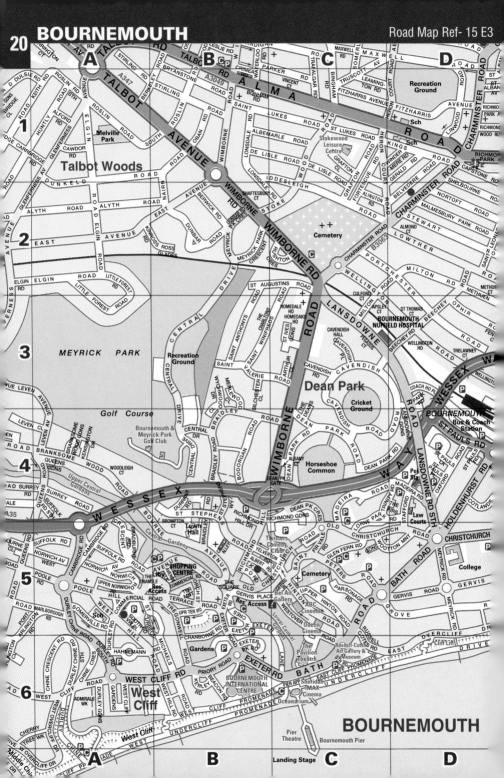

BOURNEMOUTH

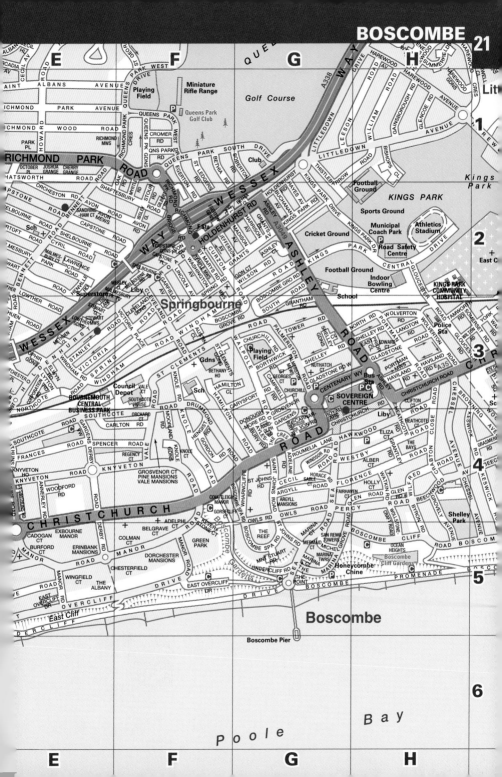

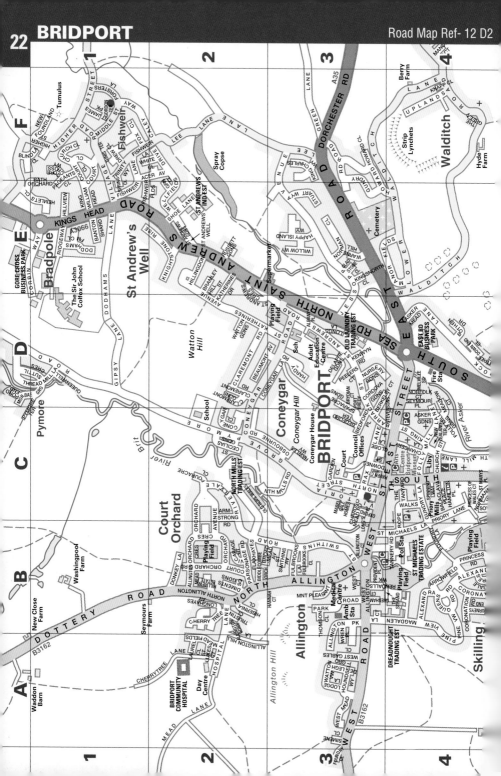

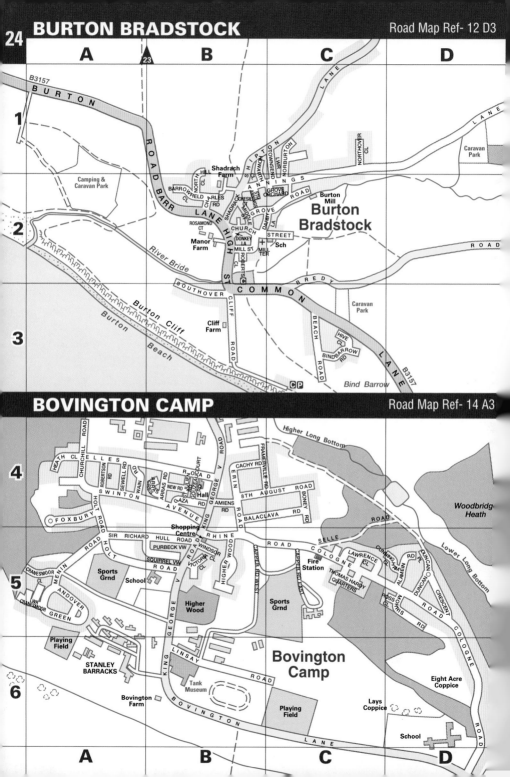

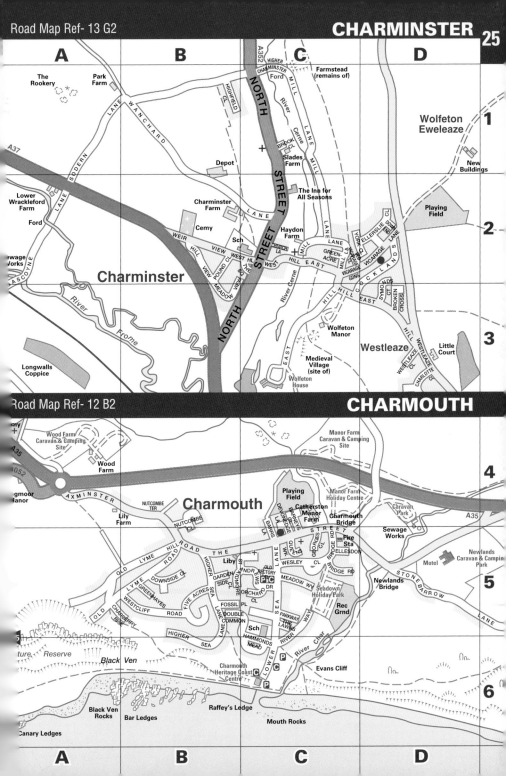

CHARMINSTER

A **B** **C** **D**

The Rookery

Park Farm

HIGHFIELD CL

A352 HIGHER CHARMINSTER Ford

Farmstead (remains of)

NORTH STREET

MILL LANE

Cerne River

Wolfeton Eweleaze

1

WANCHARD LANE

Depot

Slades Farm

BROOK CL

New Buildings

A37

SODERN LANE

Charminster Farm

The Inn for All Seasons

Playing Field

Lower Wrackleford Farm

Ford

Cemy

Sch

Haydon Farm

LANE MILL

YORK GDNS

ELLERSLIE CL

VICARAGE

DOWN LANE

2

GASCOYNE

WEIR

HILL VIEW

WEST HL

CHURCH LA

WEST

Haydon Farm

GREEN-ACRE

VICARAGE GDNS

COCKLANDS

SYMONDS CT

BROKEN CROSS

ewage Works

POUND CL

THE MEADOW

VIEW

HILL EAST

River Cerne

HILL HILL EAST

Charminster

River Frome

NORTH

EAST

Wolfeton Manor

WESTLEAZE CL

Westleaze

CHARLOTTE CL

Little Court

3

Longwalls Coppice

Medieval Village (site of)

Wolfeton House

CHARMOUTH

Wood Farm Caravan & Camping Site

A35

Manor Farm Caravan & Camping Site

4

A4052

gmoor anor

Wood Farm

AXMINSTER

NUTCOMBE TER

Charmouth

Playing Field

Catherston Manor Farm

Charmouth Bridge

Manor Farm Holiday Centre

Caravan Park

A35

Lily Farm

NUTCOMBE CL

BARNES LA

DEVONEDGE LA

STREET

Charmouth Bridge

Sewage Works

OLD LYME ROAD

HILL ROAD

HIGHER

THE STREET

Liby

OLD RECTORY

ST ANDREWS

WESLEY CL

GEORGES CL

Fire Sta

ELLESDON

BRIDGE RD

Newlands Caravan & Camping Park

Motel

DOWNSIDE CL

GARDEN SIDE

P C

MEADOW WY

STONE BARROW

Newlands Bridge

5

GREENHAYES

FIVE ACRES

ORCHARD CL

DR

SEA LANE

Seadown Holiday Park

LANE

WESTCLIFF

CHARBERRY RISE

FOSSIL PL

DOUBLE COMMON

PARKWAY

THE LAWNS

Rec Grnd

OLD

HIGHER

ROAD

SEA

Sch

HAMMONDS MEAD

LOWER SEA LANE

River Char

ature Reserve

Black Ven

Charmouth Heritage Coast Centre

C

P

River Char

Evans Cliff

6

Black Ven Rocks

Bar Ledges

Raffey's Ledge

Mouth Rocks

Canary Ledges

A **B** **C** **D**

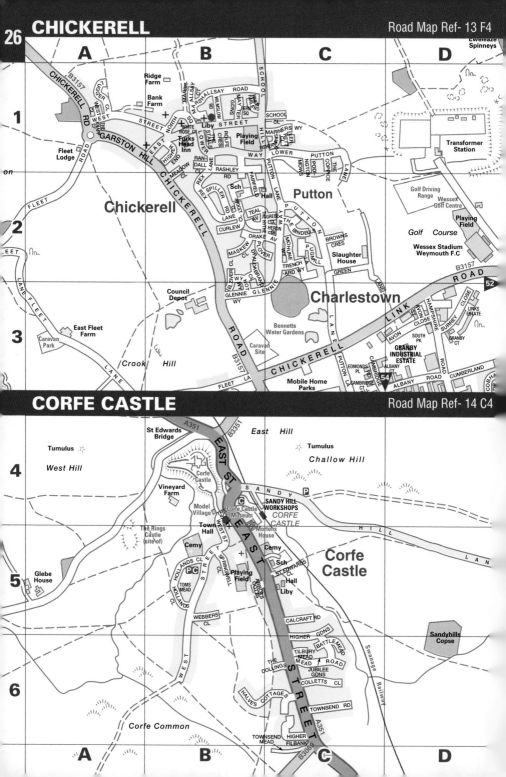

Eweleaze
Spinneys

A **B** **C** **D**

CHICKERELL RD B3157

GARSTON HILL

Ridge Farm
Bank Farm

Fleet Lodge

Liby
Turks Head Inn

Chickerell

SCHOOL ROAD

Playing Field

Putton

Transformer Station

Golf Driving Range

Wessex Golf Centre

Playing Field

Golf   Course

Wessex Stadium
Weymouth F.C

Council Depot

Slaughter House

Charlestown

B3157 ROAD

52

Bennetts Water Gardens

East Fleet Farm

Caravan Park

Crook   Hill

Caravan Site

CHICKERELL ROAD

GRANBY INDUSTRIAL ESTATE

LINKS ESTATE

GRANBY CT

54

CUMBERLAND

Mobile Home Parks

FLEET LA

A351

St Edwards Bridge

B351

East   Hill

Tumulus

Tumulus

Challow Hill

West Hill

Corfe Castle

Vineyard Farm

EAST ST

SANDY

SANDY HILL WORKSHOPS

CORFE CASTLE

HILL LAN

Model Village

Corfe Castle Museum

The Rings Castle (site of)

Town Hall

Mortons House

Cemy

Cemy

Sch

Corfe Castle

Glebe House

Playing Field

St Edwards
Hall
Liby

Sandyhills Copse

WEST STREET

EAST STREET

CALCRAFT RD

HIGHER   GDNS

BATTLE MEAD

Swanage Railway

THE DOLLINGS

JUBILEE GDNS

COLLETTS CL

TOWNSEND RD

Corfe Common

TOWNSEND MEAD

HIGHER FILBANK

A351

B3069

4

5

6

A **B** **C** **D**

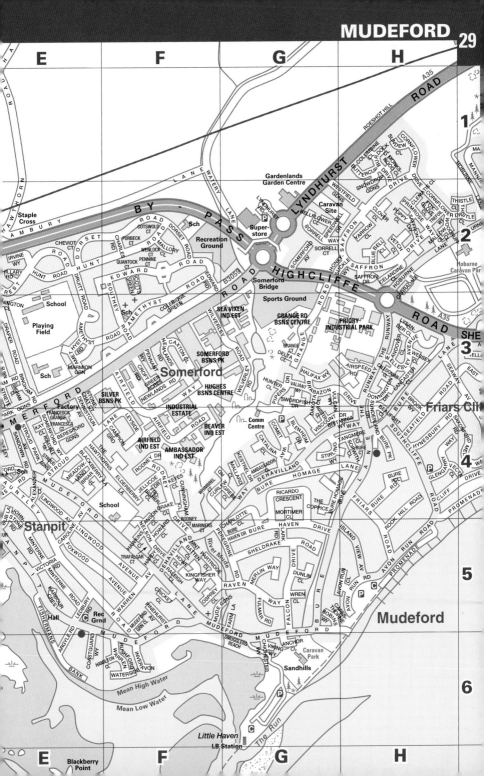

E F G H

A35

1

ROESHOT HILL

ROAD

LYNDHURST

BY-PASS ROAD

WATERY LANE

LANE

Gardenlands
Garden Centre

Lyndhurst
Gdns

Caravan
Site

Staple
Cross

HAWTHORN

AMBURY

Sch

Recreation
Ground

Superstore

Westfield

COLUMBINE
SANDVIEW CL
CORNFLOWER
BUTTERCUP DR
ROCK DRIVE
SNOWDROP
GDNS

CLEMATIS
CORNFLOWER DR
PRIMROSE WAY
POPPY CL
SAFFRON CL
MALLOW CL
SAFFRON LANE

THISTLE
CL
THE OFFSTE

2

CHEVIOT CT
COTSWOLD CT
DORSET ROAD
PURBECK CT
CHARLES RD
QUANTOCK CT
WENLOCK CT
PENNINE CT
MALLORY CT

Dorset
Road

Sch

BELLFLOWER
BUCKLE
SORRELL
SPEEDWELL

CLOVER
VETCH

YARROW CL

BLUE BELL

HONEY
SUCKLE
SAFFRON

CELANDINE

Hoburne
Caravan Par

Irvine
WY

Hillary
REST

HUNT ROAD

DRUITT ROAD
EDWARD

SOUTHEY

EDWARD
GREEN

AMETHYST

COLEBERGE
GREEN

B3059

Somerford
Bridge

SORRELL
AV

HIGHCLIFFE

SAFFRON
DR

HOBURNE
CARRIBEAN

ROAD

A35

SHE

3

NINGTON
CL

School

Playing
Field

Sch

MARMION
GRN

AMETHYST ROAD

Sch

Somerford

PENNANT

CAXTON CT
NEWLANDS
GREEN ACRES
NEWLANDS RD

AIRFIELD LANE

Factory

SILVER
BSNS PK

STROUD PARK AV

SANDOWN

DRAPER ROAD

SINNA

BINGHAM RD

MERFORD

FRANCESCA
GRANGE
SOMERFORD
GDNS
BERESFORD
GDNS

KAY CL

SYDNEY CL
DENNISTOUN AV

THE HAWTHORNS

LEYSIDE

CAMPION CL

SEA VIXEN
IND EST

WILVERLEY

SOMERFORD
BSNS PK

HUGHES
BSNS CENTRE

INDUSTRIAL
ESTATE

AIRFIELD
IND EST

AMBASSADOR
IND EST

RODNEY DR

GRANGE RD
BSNS CENTRE

GRANGE

DELTA

HUNTER

WILVERLEY WAY

Sports Ground

PRIORY
INDUSTRIAL PARK

HALIFAX WY

VALIANT
PIPERS
SWORDFISH

HAVEN

AIRSPEEDY
RD

COMET CL

BLENHEM

CATALINA
CL

AMBASSADOR
DR

BABAZON
DRIVE

VISCOUNT
DR

STIRLING

THE RUNWAY

DONNINGTON

LANCASTER
DONHEAD

CALEDONIAN

THE WELLES

BEAUFORT

SUNDERLAND

BURTON

WESSEX

SEAFIELD

HYNESBURY

Friars Clif

4

KAY CL

MUDEFORD

MEADOW CT
BRIAR CL

BLACKBERRY LA

ELDERBERRY

PELLICOE CT
RODNEY DR

KEYES
CUNNINGHAM

RODNEY
DRIVE

WIMBREL
CURLEW CL

MALLARD
KESTREL DR

GREEN CL

DEHAVILLAND

HOMAGE

STIRLING

TANGMERE
CT
HORNET CT

BURE

THE

LANE

THE COPPICE

FRIARS

BURE

BURE

HYNESBURY

SAXONHURST

GLENGARRY

AVON VALLEY
DRIVE

5

Stanpit

ALEXANDER

LINGWOOD AV

CAROLINE

LINGWOOD

THE

HAWTHORNS

School

HAWKINS

NELSON
DRIVE

HOWARD
CL

DEHAVILLAND

RODNEY

CHARLOTTE
CL
BURE CL

MARINERS
CL

HAVEN DR

RICARDO
CRESCENT

MORTIMER
CL

HOMAGE

BURE HOMAGE LA

ISLAND

VIEW AV

AVON RUN

AVON RUN RD

ROOK HILL ROAD

AVON RUN

RUN

AVON

PROMENADE

CLIFF

PROMENADE

Mudeford

JOHN

MINTERNE RD

VICTORIA

MINTERNE

RD

FOXWOOD

WARREN

TRAFALGAR
CL

KINGSTON

RALEIGH

HARTSIDE
CL

HOME
CL

RIVER WAY

HAVEN GDNS

DR

PENFOLD

KINGFISHER
WAY

MERLIN WAY

SHELDRAKE

DUNLIN
CL

DRIVE

LARK
WAY

WREN
CL

ROBINS

CARAVAN
PARK

C

Sch

JAUNTLEY

FISHERMANS BANK

HALL

HANOVER
GDNS

LEDBURY

Rec
Grnd

MUDEFORD

RUSHFORD
WARREN

WATERSIDE

HAMILTON

CRICKET
LANE

FINEHURST RD

MUDEFORD

INNER AVON

CL

FARM LA

MUDE GDNS

SMUGGLERS
REACH

CHICHESTER

VIKING
WAY

ANCHOR
CL

OSPREY
CL

RAVEN

FULMAR RD

FALCON WAY

AVON

DRIVE

Sandhills

C

P

Stanpit

Blackberry
Point

Little Haven
LB Station

The Run

C

Mean High Water

Mean Low Water

E F G H

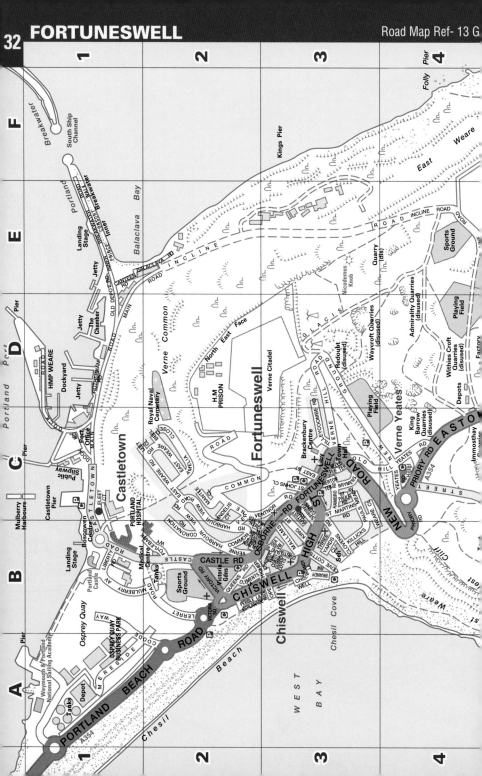

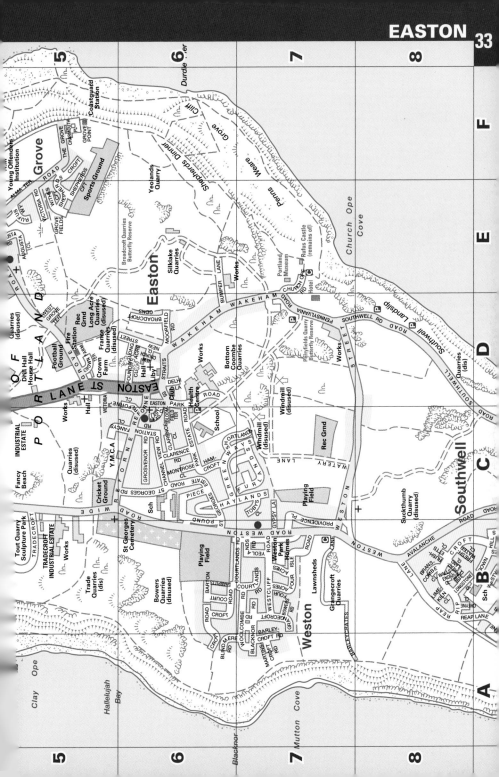

Young Offenders Institution
Coastguard Station
Grove Point
Grove
THE GROVE
CHARMOUTH PL
VICTORIA RD
ALMA TER
AUGUSTA RD
WEST GROVE TER
GROVE FIELDS
SHEPHERDS CROFT
WITHIES CL
Sports Ground
Broadcroft Quarries
Butterfly Reserve
Durdle ...er
Grove Cliff
Weare
Penns
Shepherds Dinner
Yeolands Quarry
Easton
Silklake Quarries
Church Ope Cove
Rufus Castle (remains of)
Portland Museum
Hotel
BUMPER LANE
WAKEHAM
Works
CHURCH OPE RD
PENNSYLVANIA ROAD
P
SOUTHWELL RD
Landslip
Southwell Road
Southwell
Quarries (disused)
Broadcroft Quarries Butterfly Reserve
MOORFIELD
BROADCROFT GDNS
Long Acre Quarries (disused)
Franke Quarries (disused)
Rec Grnd
Fire Station
Football Ground
Drill Hall
House Hall
QUARRIES (disused)
P O R T L A N D R O A D
P O F
WEST GROVE TER
Crown Farm
LONG ACRE
FOUNDRY CL
FANCY HILL
Hall
NEW STREET
THE STRAITS
DELHI ST
Bottom Coombe Quarries
Perryfields Quarry Butterfly Reserve
Works
STREET
Quarries (dis)
ROAD SOUTHWELL
WEST GROVE TER
C
D
E
F
INDUSTRIAL ESTATE
EASTON ST
E A S T O N
Works
Hall
Y.M.C.A.
Quarries (disused)
VICTORIA RD
STATION
GROVE RD
FANCYS
REFORNE
REFORNE
GL
EASTON SQ
Health Centre
Club
FIELD
BLOOM RD
CLIFF
PARK
School
ROAD
Windmill (disused)
Windmill (disused)
Rec Grnd
WATERY LANE
Fancy Beach
Cricket Ground
Quarries (disused)
WIDE STREET
REFORNE RD
GROSVENOR RD
CHANNEL
ST GEORGES RD
CLARENCE RD
CLARENCE RD
MONTROSE PARK
VIEW RD
ESTATE ROAD
PIECE
HAM-CROFT
PORTLANDS
CLARENCE
FURLANDS
GREENWAYS
WESTON
GYPSY LA
PROVIDENCE PL
Playing Field
Suckthumb Quarry (disused)
Southwell
A
B
C
Tout Quarry Sculpture Park
TRADECROFT
TRADECROFT INDUSTRIAL ESTATE
Works
Trade Quarries (dis)
St Georges Cemetery
Sch
HAYLANDS
PIECE
ST GEORGES
POUND ST
WEST STREET
Sch
Playing Field
Bowers Quarries (disused)
BARTON CROFT ROAD
COURT ROAD
BLINDMERE RD
WOOLCOMBE RD
BLACKNOR RD
MARTINS CROFT RD
BARLEY CROFT RD
WESTCLIFF RD
COURTLANDS RD
AMCROFT RD
FOUR ACRES
GRV
BARLEYCRATES LANE
Weston
Lawnsheds
Weston Park Homes
YEOL CL
FOUR ACRES
ISLE RD
Grangecroft Quarries
AVALANCHE LANE
WESTON ROAD
WESTON LANE
FLINTCOMBE
CLAY WALLS
PITS
BRANS... PITS
ENDS
LONGSTONE
BROWN
OAK WALK
LIME KILN
R I P
REAP LANE
CHENE RD
CROFT
FREE... PITS
REAP LANE
Sch
Clay Ope
Hallelujah Bay
Blacknor
Mutton Cove

5   6   7   8

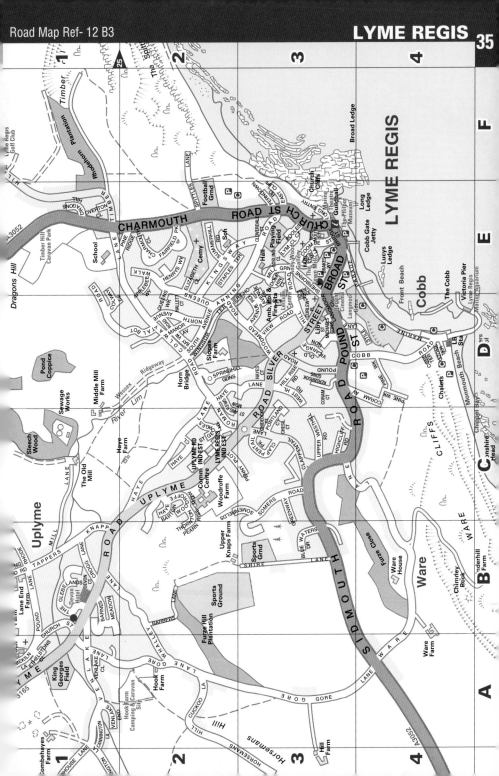

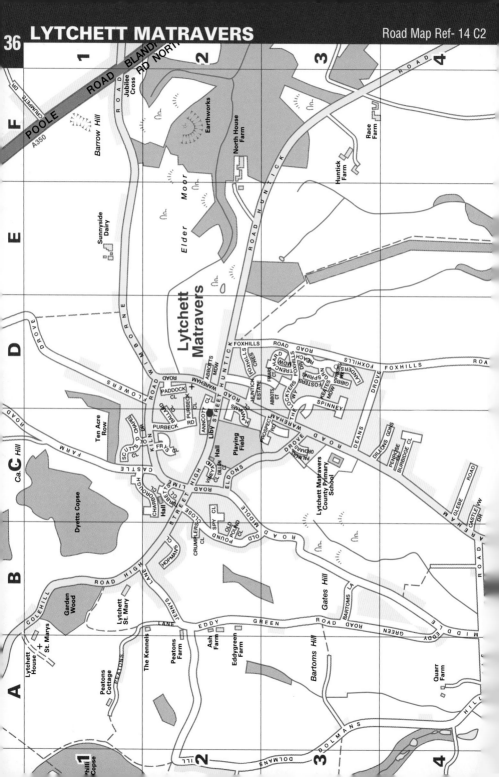

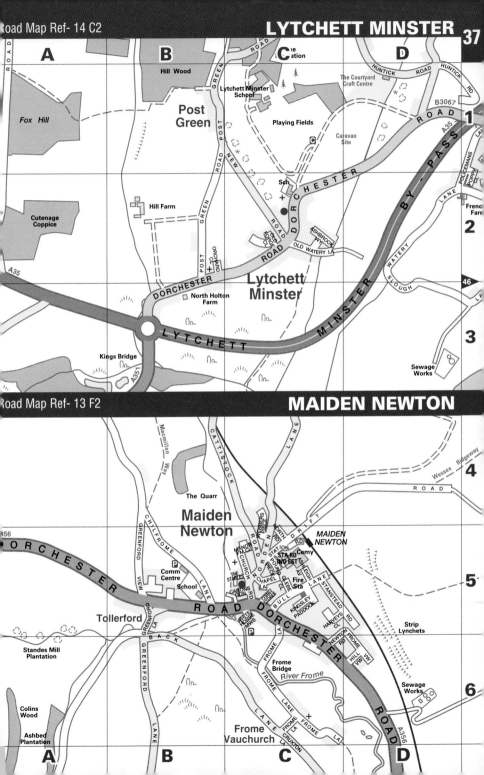

A   B   C   D

Hill Wood

Fox Hill

Post Green

Lytchett Minster School

Playing Fields

The Courtyard Craft Centre

Caravan Site

B3067

HUNTICK ROAD

HUNTICK RD

ROAD

1

POLCEMANS LANE

POPPY

Frenc Farm

Cutenage Coppice

Hill Farm

Sch

DORCHESTER ROAD

ASHBROOK WY

OLD WATERY LA

CHESTER ROAD

BY - PASS

A35

WATERY SLOUGH

2

46

A35

DORCHESTER ROAD

OLD ORCHARD

POST GREEN ROAD

NEW POST GREEN ROAD

North Holton Farm

Lytchett Minster

MINSTER

3

LYTCHETT

Kings Bridge

A351

Sewage Works

Macmillan Way

CATTISTOCK LANE

Wessex Ridgeway

4

ROAD

The Quarr

Maiden Newton

MAIDEN NEWTON

A456

DORCHESTER

CHILFROME LANE

GREENFORD VIEW

MANOR FM CL

CHURCH ROAD

NORTH STREET

CRITH LANE

DRIFT LANE

STATION RD

STA RD IND EST

Cemy

Comm Centre

School

P

THE STABLES

CANONS

CHAPEL LANE

CROSS GLEBE

BRIDGE

BULL LANE

Fire Sta

STANSTEAD RD

HARVEYS CL

HELYAR

5

ROAD

Tollerford

GREENFORD LA

BACK LANE

MYRTLE HOUSE MWS

P

COURT HOUSES

KINGSLEY PADDOCK

NEWTON FROME RD

HILL VW

Strip Lynchets

Standes Mill Plantation

FROME LANE

Frome Bridge

River Frome

DORCHESTER ROAD

Sewage Works

6

Colins Wood

FROME LANE

Frome Vauchurch

FROME LA FROME

CRUXTON LA

A356

Ashbed Plantation

A   B   C   D

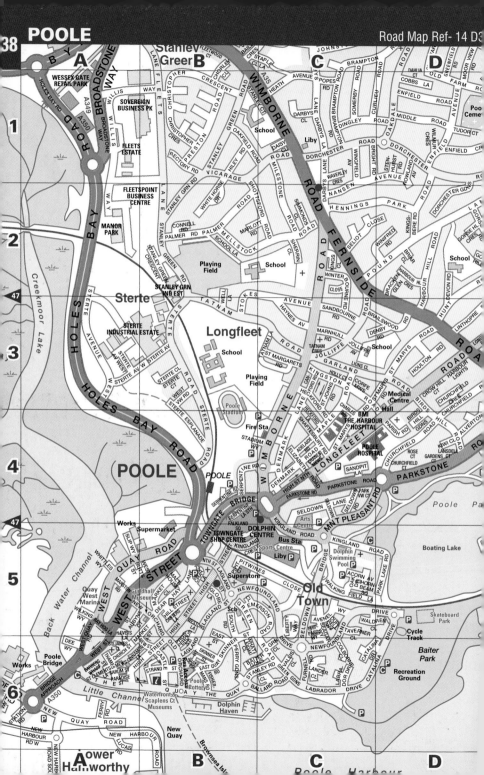

PRESTON

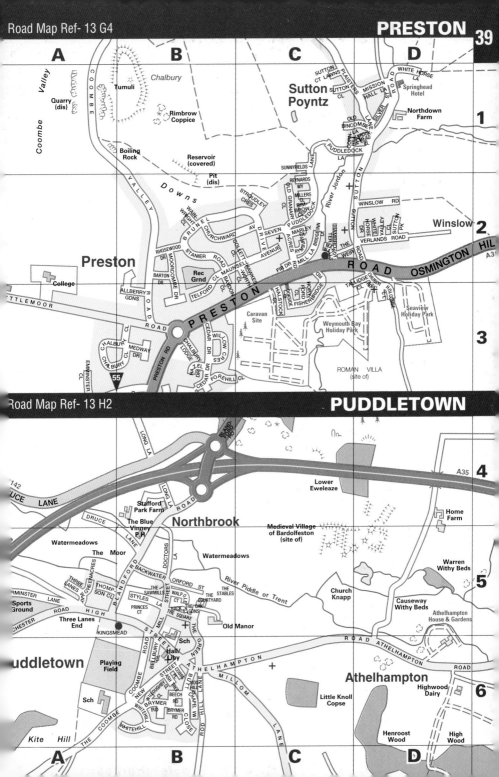

A **B** **C** **D**

1

Coombe Valley

Quarry (dis)

Chalbury

Tumuli

Rimbrow Coppice

Boiling Rock

Reservoir (covered)

Pit (dis)

Downs

Sutton Poyntz

WHITE HORSE LA

Springhead Hotel

Northdown Farm

SUTTON CT LAWNS
PLAISTERS CL
MISSION HALL LA
OLD BINCOMBE
SILVER ST
PUDDLEDOCK LA
SUTTON RD

SUNNYFIELDS

REYNARDS WY
MILLERS
BROW
OLD GRANARY
PUDDLEDOCK

River Jordan

WINSLOW RD

Winslow
2

STROUDLEY CRES
WAINE WRIGHT
BRUNEL
CHURCHWARD
STANIER
COLLETT
MAUNSELL
AV
DRIVE
SEVEN ACRES
MARLEY LA
FIR DR
MILL LA
WRIGHT
BRIDGEINN

WINSLOW DR
WHITE HORSE
VERLANDS
VALLEY
SUTTON PK
SUTTON ROAD
THE

Preston

RHOSEWOOD DR
MOORCOMBE DR
BARTON DR
Rec Grnd
TELFORD CL
BARDON
WILLOW CRES
HALSTOCK CL

WEIR
OLD
HORTH FOND
FISHERBRIDGE
BRIDGMORE
TALLIDGE
CHURCH CL
HILLCOMBE CT

R O A D   OSMINGTON HIL
A3

College

ALLBERRY GDNS

P R E S T O N

Caravan Site

Weymouth Bay Holiday Park

Seaview Holiday Park
3

TTLEMOOR

CHALBURY CL
MEDWAY DR
CHALBURY CL
EMINSTER CL

CEDAR DR
CHALBURY LODGE
EL
CEDAR DR
FOREHILL CL
WILLOW CRES

PRESTON RD
ROAD

ROMAN VILLA (site of)

55

PUDDLETOWN

BILAND RD

LONG LA

A35
4

RUCE LANE

DRUCE

LONG LA ROAD

Stafford Park Farm

The Blue Vinney P.H

Northbrook

Lower Eweleaze

Medieval Village of Bardolfeston (site of)

Home Farm

Watermeadows

The Moor

DOCTORS LA
BACKWATER

ORFORD ST

Watermeadows

River Piddle or Trent

Warren Withy Beds
5

THREE LANES WAY
THOMPSON CL
BLANDFORD
THE SAWMILLS
STYLES
PRINCES CT
THE SQUARE
THE OAK
THE STABLES
COURTYARD
THE GDNS

Church Knapp

Causeway Withy Beds

Athelhampton House & Gardens

RMINSTER LANE
Sports Ground
CHESTER
ROAD

Three Lanes End
KINGSMEAD

HIGH ST
BELBURY
MILL STREET
THE GREEN
ATHELHAMPTON

Old Manor

Puddletown

Playing Field

Sch

Hall Liby

Sch

NEW
WILLOUGHBY
COOMBE
BUTT
BEECH RD
BRYMER RD
BRYMER RD
WHITEHILL
NORTH HILL
CAPEL WI CLOSE

ATHELHAMPTON ROAD

Highwood Dairy
6

Athelhampton

Little Knoll Copse

Henroost Wood

High Wood

Kite Hill

THE COOMBE

MILLOM LANE

CAPEL LANE

A **B** **C** **D**

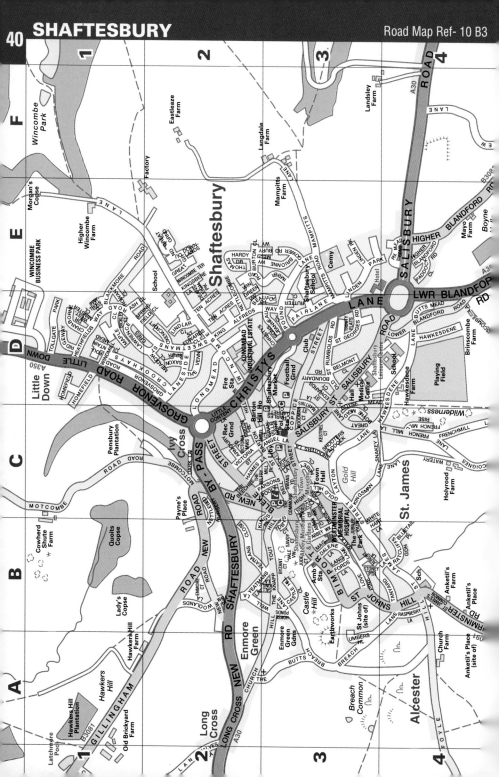

Sherborne

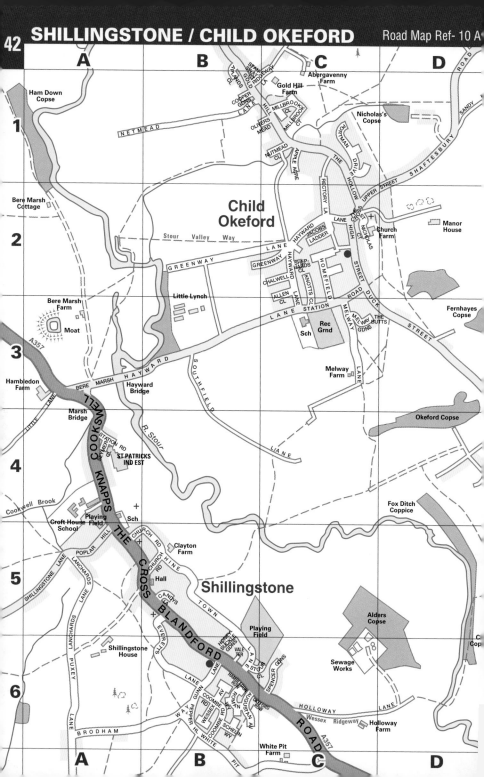

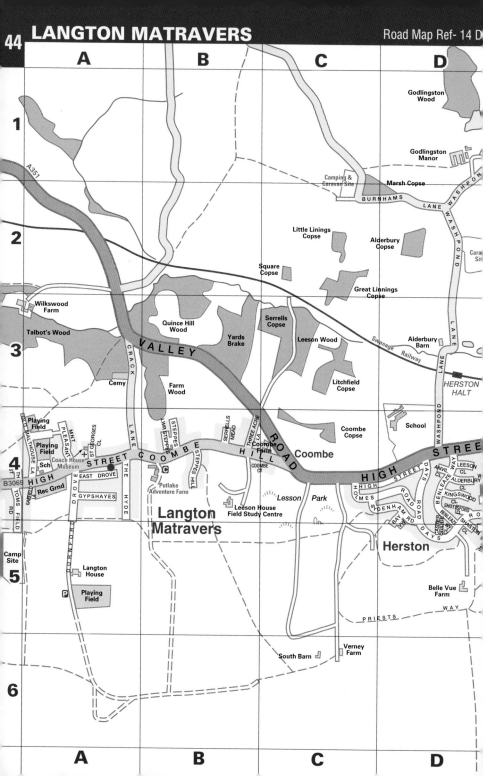

A351

Godlingston Wood

Godlingston Manor

Camping & Caravan Site

Marsh Copse

BURNHAMS LANE

WASHPOND LANE

Caravan Site

Little Linings Copse

Alderbury Copse

Square Copse

Great Linnings Copse

Wilkswood Farm

Talbot's Wood

Quince Hill Wood

VALLEY

CRACK LANE

Serrells Copse

Yards Brake

Leeson Wood

Swanage Railway

Alderbury Barn

HERSTON HALT

Cemy

Farm Wood

Litchfield Copse

School

Playing Field

Playing Field

Coach House Museum

HIGH STREET

ST GEORGES CL

MNT PLEASANT

LANE

COOMBE

STEPPES

LWR STEPPES

STEPPES HILL

SERRELLS MEAD

THREE ACRE LA

COOMBE CT

Coombe Farm

Coombe Copse

HIGH STREET

LEESON CL

ALDERBURY CL

KINGSWOOD CL

SHOTSFORD CL

ANVIL CL

BENLEASE WAY

DAYS ROAD

BENLEASH

DENHAM RD

HOLMES

HIGH

BAY

SHASTON RD

Sch

Rec Grnd

EAST DROVE

THE HYDE

Putlake Adventure Farm

Coombe

Lesson Park

Leeson House Field Study Centre

HIGH

TOMS FIELD RD

B3069

GYPSHAYES

DROVE

Langton Matravers

Herston

Camp Site

Langton House

P

Playing Field

Belle Vue Farm

WAY

PRIESTS

South Barn

Verney Farm

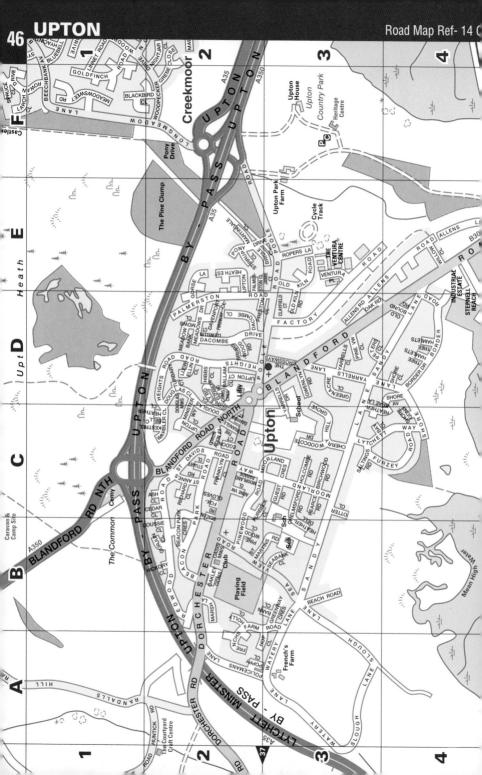

Creekmoor Lake

Holes Bay

Upton Lake

Marina

Cobbs Quay

QUAY

COBBS ROAD

WOODLANDS

WOODLAND AV

WOODLANDS ROAD

AVENUE

HINCHCLIFFE RD

HINCHCLIFFE

Superstore

BURPGATE RD

CRES

HAMILTON CRES

HAMILTON ROAD

WINSTON AVENUE

RIDSEMOUNT GDNS

UPWEY

ALMER RD

CARTERS

FRESHWATER DRIVE

FRESHWATER CRES

CARISBROOKE

DAWKINS ROAD

DAWKINS RD

DAWKINS RD

GALLOWAY RD

Fire Sta.

HEWITT RD

HEWITT RD

HEWITT ROAD

SYMES RD

SYMES RD

SYMES RD

SYMES RD

INGLESHAM WAY

HARKWOOD DRIVE

BECKHAMPTON RD

MANTON RD

MANTON RD

MANTON CL

FALCONER DR

ROAD

B L A N D F O R D

R O A D

B3068

BLANDFORD ROAD

GOATHORN ROAD

PIER

RICE GDNS

KEYSWORTH ROAD

HAMWORTHY JUNCTION

MARYLAND RD

LEBERE RD

MID CRES

FITZWORTH

GARDENS

MIDLIN

SHIPSTAL CL

RUSSELL RD

FORELAND RD

PATCHINS RD

PATCHINS

PEVERELL RD

EGMONT RD

SOUTH HAVEN

REDHORN CL

NAPIER ROAD

Sports & Recreation Ground

Schools

Turlin Moor

Community Centre

Hamworthy

Ham Hill

WALCHEREN

Rockley Sands

ROCKLEY PARK Caravan Park

NAPIER ROAD

Ham Common

Rec Ground

School

ECCLES RD

BECCLES RD

VICARAGE

ASHMORE AVENUE

TUCKERS LANE

LANARK CL

ALBANY RD

LEGION CL

LEGION CL

HOUNSLOW CL

ROCKLEY MWS

ASHMORE CRES

AVENUE

ROAD

School

Sch

Hamworthy Park

Paddling Pool

PURBECK AV

LULWORTH CLOSE

LULWORTH CRES

ROCKLEY

COLES GDNS

JACOBS ROAD

JOSHUA RD

ANNETT RD

NATHAN GDNS

DELILAH ROAD

HERCULES ROAD

SAMSON ROAD

NORMANDY

HYDE ROAD

DAVID WAY

KANGAW PL

NAPIER LAKE

ROAD

LAKE DRIVE

LAKE DRIVE

LULWORTH AVENUE

BRANKSEA AV

BRANKSEA CL

BRANKSEA AVENUE

AVENUE

Lake

MORICONIUM QUAY

Marina

Pontoons

Pier

Amphibious Training Unit Royal Marines

POOLE HARBOUR

Wareham Channel

HALTER PATH

CAPTAINS ROW

LAKE ROAD

ROADROYAL

CAVER RD

SHAM CL

LAKE CRES

GIBBS ROAD

NEW-HA

STATION

BRADWICK ROAD

The OLD ROPE WALK

B3068

IVOR ROAD

MOORINGS

RIGLER ROAD

BLANDFORD ROAD

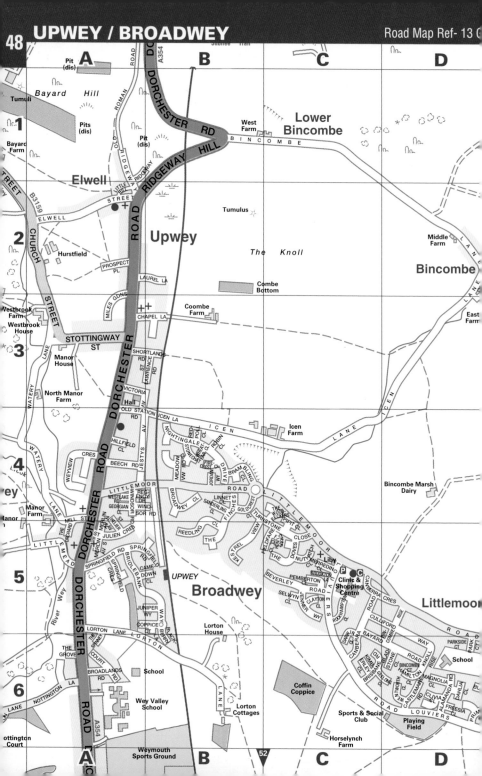

A **B** **C** **D**

Pit (dis)

Tumuli

Bayard Hill

Pits (dis)

Bayard Farm

West Farm

1

Lower Bincombe

Pit (dis)

BINCOMBE

Elwell

RIDGEWAY

RIDGEWAY HILL

DORCHESTER RD

A354

ROMAN ROAD

LITTLE HILL STREET

Upwey

Tumulus

Middle Farm

2

CHURCH STREET

ELWELL STREET

Hurstfield

PROSPECT PL

The Knoll

Bincombe

Westbrook Farm

Westbrook House

STREET

LANE

MILES GDNS

LAUREL LA

Combe Bottom

East Farm

3

STOTTINGWAY ST

CHAPEL LA

Coombe Farm

Manor House

North Manor Farm

WATERY LANE

SHORTLANDS RD

LAWRENCE RD

VICTORIA

Old Station RD

Hall

ICEN LA

DORCHESTER ROAD

ICEN

Icen Farm

ICEN LANE

4

WATERY

Manor Farm

WEYVIEW CRES

HILLFIELD CL

BEECH RD

JESTYS AV

NIGHTINGALE CL

MEADOW VW

STONE CL

RED POLL

ROBIN CL

FIRE CRESS

JORDAN

BRAMBLING

Bincombe Marsh Dairy

ey

Manor Farm

THE EMEAD

MILL ST

LITTLE

LITTLEMOOR

WESTLAKE RD

GEORGIAN DR

TREE FARM

WIND- SOR RD

BROADWEY CL

DRIVE

MEADOW

ROAD

LINNET CL

SANDERLING CL

FINCHES

GOLDCREST

LITTLEMOOR ROAD

THE

PIPIT CL

TURNSTONE

KESTREL

DOVES

NUTHATCH

Lib

P C

Clinic & Shopping Centre

5

River Wey

SPRINGFIELD RD

SPRINGFIELD CRES

BRIDLEBANK

CAMEL DOWN

REEDLING

THE

UPWEY

Broadwey

FELDFARE

VIEW

CLOSE

SELWYN CL

BEVERLEY

PEMBERTON

JENNER WY

CLAYTON CL

ROAD

ROXHAMPTON

VIVIERS

CANBERRA CRES

CULLIFORD

BAYARD

STONE

BINCOMBE

KNOLL

RISE

Littlemoor

ROAD

WAY

PARKSIDE CT

6

NOTTINGTON LA

THE GROVE

COURT

JUNIPER WY

COPPICE

BLACK BERRY

LORTON LANE

BROADLANDS RD

School

Wey Valley School

Lorton House

Lorton Cottages

Coffin Coppice

Sports & Social Club

Horselynch Farm

DAW LN

CATBERRA

KINGS RD

BRISBANE

CASTLEMAN

WENTWORTH

LOUVIERS

HAMILTON CL

MAGNOLIA RD

CLIVIA

ALAMANDA CL

DAHLIA

FREESIA

School

Playing Field

ottington Court

Weymouth Sports Ground

Weymouth Sports Ground

A **B** **52** **C** **D**

48

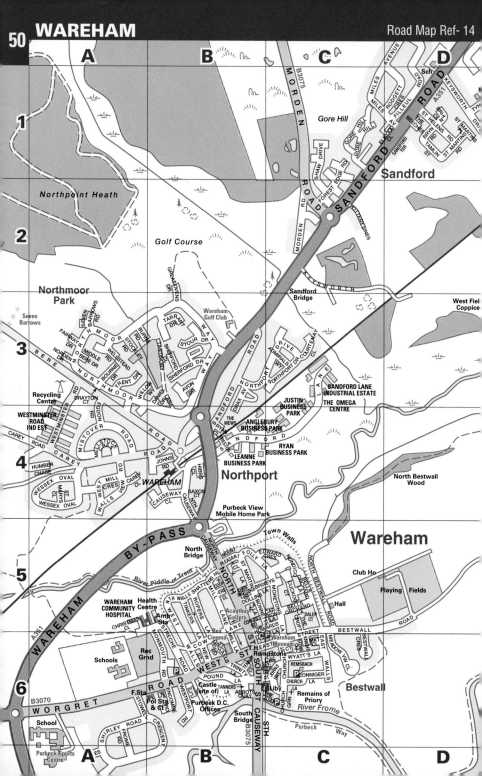

WAREHAM

Sandford

Wareham

Northport

Bestwall

Northpoint Heath

Northmoor Park

Golf Course

Gore Hill

Sandford Bridge

West Fiel Coppice

Wareham Golf Club

Seven Barrows

Recycling Centre

WESTMINSTER ROAD IND EST

SANDFORD LANE INDUSTRIAL ESTATE

THE OMEGA CENTRE

JUSTIN BUSINESS PARK

ANGLEBURY BUSINESS PARK

RYAN BUSINESS PARK

LEANNE BUSINESS PARK

THE MEWS

HUMBER CHASE

North Bestwall Wood

Purbeck View Mobile Home Park

Town Walls

WAREHAM COMMUNITY HOSPITAL

Health Centre

North Bridge

Schools

Rec Grnd

Amb Sta

Club Ho

Playing Fields

Hall

Acanthus Gallery

Cinema

Wareham Museum

Rampstone Cen

Castle (site of)

F.Sta

Pol Sta & Ct

Purbeck D.C. Offices

South Bridge

Remains of Priory

River Frome

Purbeck Way

School

Purbeck Sports Centre

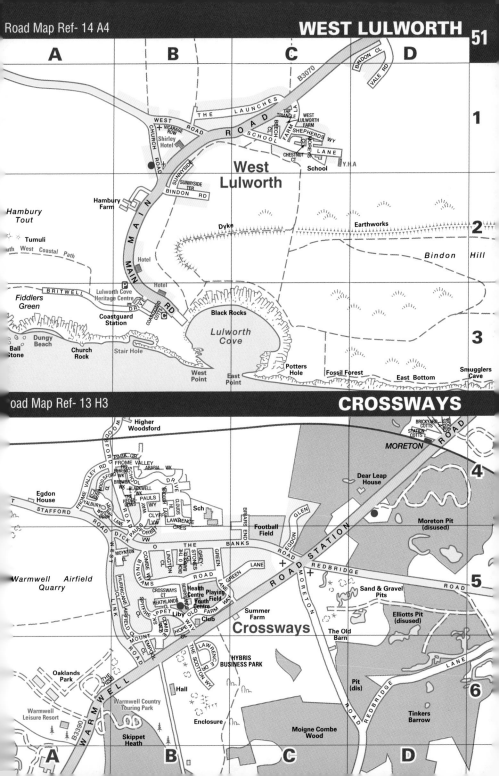

A **B** **C** **D**

1

WEST ROAD
CHURCH ROAD
VICARAGE ROW
Shirley Hotel
THE LAUNCHES
ROAD
SCHOOL
THE TRIANGLE
BEECH
FARM LA
WEST LULWORTH FARM
SHEPHERDS WY
MOREYS LANE
CHESTNUT CT
School
Y.H.A
BINDON CL
VALE RD
B3070

SUNNYSIDE
SUNNYSIDE TER
BINDON RD
West Lulworth

Hambury Farm

Hambury Tout

Tumuli

uth West Coastal Path

MAIN ROAD

Hotel

Dyke

Earthworks

Bindon Hill

2

Fiddlers Green

BRITWELL

Lulworth Cove Heritage Centre

COASTGUARD COTTS

DR Y

MAIN RD

Coastguard Station

Black Rocks

Lulworth Cove

3

Ball Stone

Dungy Beach

Church Rock

Stair Hole

West Point

East Point

Potters Hole

Fossil Forest

East Bottom

Smugglers Cave

Higher Woodsford

BRICKYARD COTTS
STATION COTTS
MORETON
ROAD

4

Egdon House

STAFFORD

FROME VALLEY RD
WOODSFORD RD
PARK DR
FROME VALLEY
ABARIA
WK
BLACKWELL WK
THE HEDGE ROWS
ST PAULS WY
CLYFFE
DRIVE
WRIGHT WK
CLOUDS HL
LAWRENCE CRES
Sch
BRIAR END
GLEN
Dear Leap House
Moreton Pit (disused)

EGDON ROAD

ROAD

Football Field

Sand & Gravel Pits

5

Warmwell Airfield Quarry

WEST ROAD
DICK ST PAULS
MOYNTON CL
BINGHAMS
HURRICANE AIRFIELD LINK
COMBE WY
LINGTON CL
GREY STONES
THE GREEN
BANKS
LANE
ROAD

STATION ROAD
MORETON

REDBRIDGE

ROAD

Elliotts Pit (disused)

CROSSWAYS CT
HEATHLANDS
SPITFIRE RD
SKIPPET CL
EMPICK
Health Centre
Youth Centre
Playing Field
Club
Summer Farm
The Old Barn
OLD FARM WY
HOPE RD
Liby
Crossways

Pit (dis)

6

Oaklands Park

WARMWELL
MOUNT ROAD
THE RISE
LAWRENCE
THE SCOTION WY
Hall
HYBRIS BUSINESS PARK

Enclosure

Moigne Combe Wood

REDBRIDGE LANE

ROAD

Tinkers Barrow

Warmwell Leisure Resort

B3390

Warmwell Country Touring Park

Skippet Heath

A **B** **C** **D**

E **F** **G** **H**

Field

Wyke Oliver Farm

Overcombe

Horse Lynch Plantation

Jordan Hill

New Barn

1

Jordan Hill Roman Temple (remains of)

COVEWAY

Bowl

BRACKENDOWN

AVENUE

EASTDOWN

MOORDOWN

SOUTHDOWN

Hide

Playground

RADLEY CT

KEAST CT

Overcombe Court

Furzy Cliff

2

Lodmoor Nature Reserve (RSPB)

PRESTON BEACH ROAD

ESPLANADE

Waste Centre

3

Miniature Golf Course

Lodmoor Country Park

Miniature Railway

Sea Life Centre

Aquarium & Butterfly Farm

Pirate Adventure Golf

Sk8 Park

BAY

4

Sch

Sports Ground

Melcombe Regis

P.H.

College

GREENHILL

Rowland

Greenhill Gardens

STANTON CT

WEYMOUTH

5

WEYMOUTH COMMUNITY HOSPITAL

Trimar Hospice

WESTERHALL Road

DORCHESTER Road

WEYMOUTH BAY

6

Jubilee Clock

E **F** **G** **H**

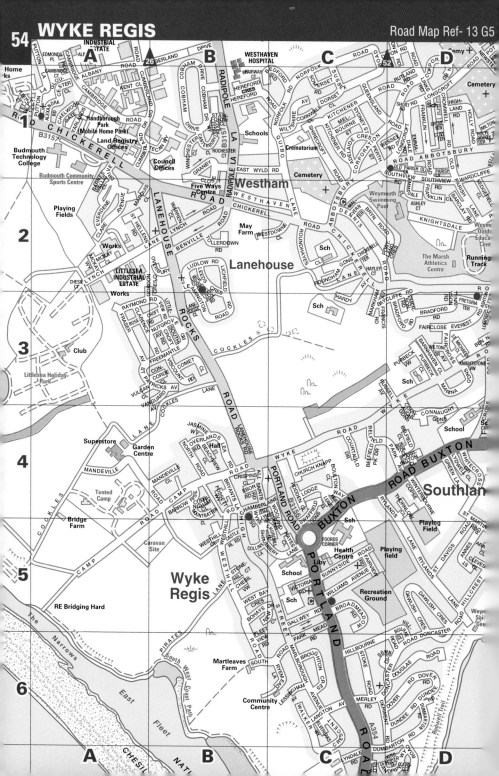

WEYMOUTH

Rodwell

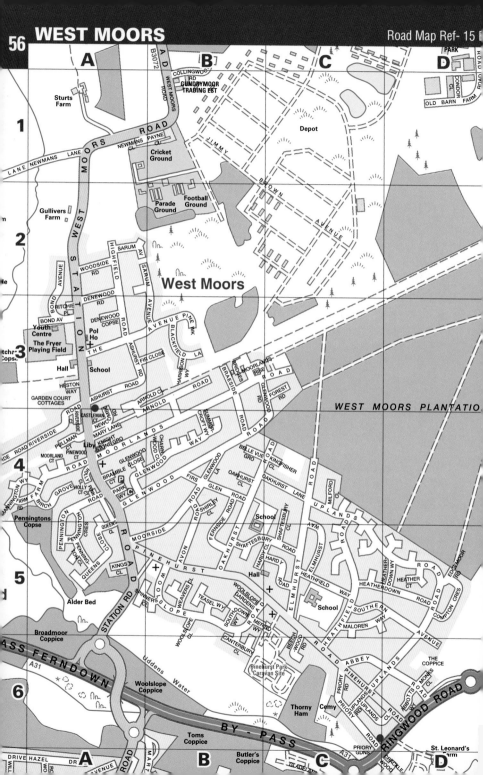

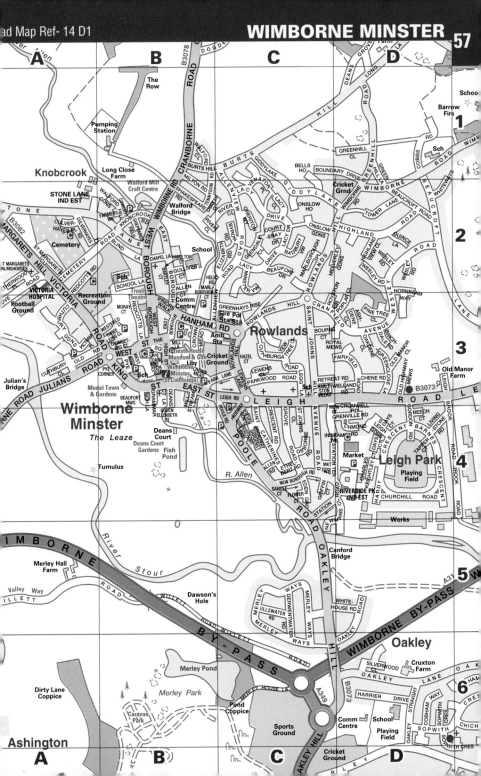

A B C D

1

Woolbridge Manor
Footbridge
River Frome
Wool Bridge
WAREHAM ROAD
A352
East Burton Dairy
WATER MEADOW LA
The Moors
WOODBRIDGE BUSINESS CENTRE
Caravan & Camping Site
WOOL
MORETON RD
SANDHILLS CRES
East Burton
EAST BURTON ROAD
THE ALISONS
BURTON
FAIRFIELDS
STATION RD
HYDE
BINDON
2

GIDDY GRN LA
Giddy Green
BAILEYS
AVE
LAMPTON CL
BURTON CL
SYDENHAM CRES
Sch
Rec Grnd
HIGH
HYDE RD
LOCKS CT
JER CL
BINDON CROSS
THE
Wool
Manor Farm
BURTON RD
GIDDY GRN RD
FROME
DROVE
SYDENHAM
COTTAGE CL
SWALLOW
LINCLETH RD
FOLLY LA
D'Urberville Centre & Liby
Youth Centre
BEACH
LANDON
CLOSE
SPRINGHILL
CHURCH
Braytown
CHALK PIT LANE
COLLIERS
KNOWLE WOOD
KNAP
KNOWLE HILL
Sch
Access to Winfrith Technology Park
DORCHESTER ROAD
OAKDENE RD
GARAGE LA
HILLSIDE
LOWER HILLSIDE
Watercress Beds
LULWORTH RD
B3071

3

A352
DORCHESTER RD
NEW BUILDINGS RD
Burton Cross
HILLSIDE
BURTON WOOD
NEW RD
CHARR HILL
MCCAULEY LANE

INDEX TO STREETS
with Postcodes

The Index includes some names for which there is insufficient space on the maps. These names are indicated by an * and are followed by the nearest adjoining thoroughfare.